Molasses and Midges

Diaries of Granny Irving

A short history of a large family

Evy Irving

ISBN: 978-1-968296-79-7 Evelyn D. Hunck-Irving

Table of Contents

Dedication i

Acknowledgement.. ii

About the Author iii

*How We Emigrated Twice And Ended Up In the Highlands of
Scotland* 1

1943.. 3

    January 24: 3

    February 23: 3

    September 17: 3

1944 - 1951 4

Back to Scotland.. 7

1953.. 10

1954.. 13

    January – March.. 13

    April 14

    May 16

    June 19

    July... 24

    August 26

    September 29

    October.. 31

    December 40

    Sunday 26 Dec '54 42

1955 January 43

    February 44

    Monday 21 Feb '55 45

    March 45

    April 45

    May 46

    June 46

Monday 13 June '55.. 47

Conclusion **48**

Mum's Original Diary-Entries.................................. 49

1944.. 49

January 49

February 52

March 56

April 59

May 60

June 62

September 62

November... 63

December 63

Dedication

To all the Irving children. May they preserve the past while looking to the future.

Acknowledgement

To our late mum, Catherine Gladioli Irving nee Morgan, for her years of writing up diaries and keeping them.

For the many hours of digitalizing our mum's/granny's diaries, many thanks to my sisters, Elsie and Dot and niece Shirley. It is a huge amount of work and we all look forward to getting it finished.

About the Author

Evelyn was born in Dunoon, Scotland. Met her Dutch husband at 20 and since then has lived and worked in the Netherlands. With three children and six grandchildren, holding a full-time job as a secretary and management assistant, she became a sworn legal translator. Writing and reading were always Evelyn's passions, along with maintaining family ties in Scotland and spanning the globe.

How We Emigrated Twice

And

Ended Up In the Highlands of Scotland

These diaries belong to the Irving family of Scotland. After our Mum (Granny Irving—Catherine Gladioli, also known as Gladys, nee Morgan) died in October 1998, we collected her diaries on the computer so that all the family could enjoy reading them.

First, a brief family history of a large family: Mum (later also known as Gladys) was born Catherine Gladioli Morgan on 17 September 1916 in Edinburgh, Scotland, as the eldest daughter of Walter Morgan and Catherine Jane Fox McCleary. On 17 September 1943, she married our dad, Harold George Irving, a Canadian from Campbellton, New Brunswick, Canada. They settled in Edinburgh, had a son, and then emigrated to New Brunswick, Canada, in 1945. After five years (and four daughters born there), they re-migrated to Scotland, where the last five children were born. To make a book is a huge undertaking and we will do our utmost to preserve the feelings and elements that Gladys put into her writing.

Kate (Catherine) Morgan, aged 14 in 1930

[Coloured version enhanced by My Heritage.]

Farnborough provided plenty to entertain the forces when off duty. There were two cinemas, the Scala and the Rex; the Navy, Army and Air Force Institute canteen and T.O.C.H where you could get snacks. There were nice lounges with comfortable armchairs where you could sit down and rest in the evenings. Barn dances with the Canadians were popular. And of course chocolates and sweets.

The story of how Gladys and George met in Farnborough, south England, during WWII begins with a few terse notes in 1943.

1943

January 24:

I met Brick (*our dad, George—why Brick?*) and 'Shorty.'

February 23:

Brick proposed.

September 17:

We were married (*in Edinburgh, Scotland*).

Gladys & George on their Wedding Day

1944 - 1951

Bits 'n pieces from the entire period. We have no diaries saved from the period between December 1944 and June 1951. We know only what we heard from our parents or the older children. Not surprising if Gladys didn't find time to write up a diary, what with having five, then six very young children to look after.

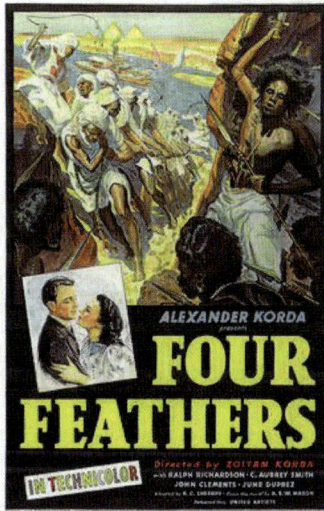

Movie poster advertisement for <u>The Four Feathers</u> - © 1939 <u>United Artists.</u>

These diaries began in January 1944, shortly after Gladys and George got married in Edinburgh. Their married life began separately in Farnborough, England, where they had first met. Separately? Yes, because they were both still in the forces. George in the Royal Canadian Regiment and Gladys in the WAAF (Women's Auxiliary Air Force). Only after Gladys was expecting their first child, did they both receive an honorary discharge, and they moved up to Gladys's family home in Edinburgh, Scotland. While in Farnborough, they often went to the pictures and saw such films as: "She Knew All the Answers," (Gladys wrote: I never even knew the questions!), a 1941 comedy film made by Columbia Pictures, and "The Four Feathers," a 1939 British Technicolor adventure film.

On leave in Edinburgh in March 1944, they bought a gramophone and records. Back down South, they took a trip to Guildford (Essex), a quaint old town where they visited fortifications dating back to 43 B.C. At the end of May, Gladys got her effective date of discharge from the WAAF. Sometime after December 1944, George also received his discharge. Back in Scotland, they arranged their emigration to Canada. Still living with Gladys' parents, they had little to pack for the trip. In August 1945, George arrived in Canada. Then on 29 April 1946, Gladys and baby Freddy arrived in Campbellton, New Brunswick, Canada, where they soon rented (or bought?) a house. Gladys seemed to get on well with her sister-in-law, our aunt Janet. We later found out there was some scandal involved, when around 2015, we were contacted by a full cousin of ours. We'd never heard of him but DNA proved he was related to us. He was born in the Ideal Maternity home in the small seaside town of East Chester in Nova Scotia. The scandal was found out by research and named the 'Butterbox Babies.' You can read about it under <u>View of Scandal and Social Policy: The Ideal Maternity Home and the Evolution of Social Policy in Nova Scotia,</u>

<u>1940-51</u> | <u>Acadiensis</u> or other places on the internet. Our cousin was one of the lucky survivors, being a blue-eyed blond baby. Here is part of his birth certificate.

FORM 4.   PROVINCE OF NOVA SCOTIA   Registered No.......
For use of Registr

CERTIFICATE OF REGISTRATION OF BIRTH
(BY PARENT OR GUARDIAN)

NOTE:—In case of more than one child at a birth, a Separate Return must be made for each, and the number of each, in order of birth

PLACE OF BIRTH.

County of *Lunenburg.*   Municipality of *Chester*

City, Town or Village *East Chester N.S* Street *Ideal Maternity Home* House No.
(If birth occurred in a hospital, give its name instead of Street and Number)

Anyway, Gladys was soon pregnant again with twins, Linda and Kay, who were born in January 1947. The next year, Susan was born and a year later, Wendy. By this time, Gladys was utterly fed-up with the extremely cold winters, with up to three metres of snow and the scorching hot summers. So, they decided to re-migrate to Scotland.

Back to Scotland

Edinburgh is where the next two children were born. Elsie in 1950 and Charlie in 1952, and it seemed to get just a bit crowded in our grandparent's house(!) with all 11 of them. Our grandma, Catherine Jane Fox McLeary, had died in 1949. Our disabled aunt Brenda (Gladys' youngest sister) lived there too. It was just a small apartment. In the summer of 1951, there were six young children, all sick with measles. George had found a job as a bus conductor in Edinburgh, but that wasn't to his liking. So he got a job in forestry in Argyll, on the west coast of Scotland and moved there with now 7 young children. He just loved the outdoors and swore he'd never go back to his first job as a bank clerk in Canada. Ten miles from Dunoon, we lived in a cottage at the edge of Loch Eck, north of Glasgow. A beautiful place, but with another two babies arriving within a couple of years (Evelyn in 1953 and Dorothy in 1954), it was a hard job to keep the family in food and clothing.

Photo of Loch Eck

Gladys often wrote little anecdotes, to which only she would know the answer. Like this one: 'Heard an amusing episode on the radio of the young flying instructor and the elderly gentleman.' I wonder what that was all about!

Now to the diaries. This is more or less just as Gladys had written it down. Edited by me (Evelyn). I will add explanations where necessary and maybe just a wee bit of my own memories when they come to mind. I hope you enjoy reading this family story.

1951

June

Measles

Monday 24 June '51 – Dr M. McDiarmid.

Elsie (the baby): her eyes have been closed for the last four days. I've sponged them open with boracic several times. She hasn't taken in more than ½ pint of milk in that time and about 1½ pints of water. Once I gave her water and orange juice, but she didn't take it. Her mouth seems sore. Her bowel movements have been frequent, but very sparse and dark green in colour, and very loose. She sleeps mostly and cries very little – very slight rash. Breathing rapid, temperature high.

Linda, 4 years: slept all through it. Attack seemed slight in comparison. Wants to get up in bed since last Tuesday.

Kay, 4 years: attack similar. Up on Saturday.

Freddie has bad sties.

Wendy, 20 months: has been asleep for the last 4 or 5 days. She cries every time she wets her sheet. She has had two bowel movements in that time – one this morning, fairly loose. Her eyes have been stuck all that time. I tried hard to get them washed and opened, but she fought me. Rash slightly off.

Susan, 3 years: sick since Wednesday. In bed since Thursday. Rash very bad up till yesterday. Very feverish. Improved today.

1953

Bits 'n pieces from the whole year.

In August '53, Evelyn was born in Dunoon in the Cottage Hospital (in the two pictures above). Later on, in December '54, Dorothy was born in the same place.

The loch is up over the road. Some cars with low exhaust pipes can't drive through. The Postman managed on foot by climbing round through the forest. I can't work for watching out the window. At 1.30 p.m., Evelyn (2 months) is asleep. Charlie (1½ years old) is asleep. I will not spoil the spell of peacefulness by investigating what mischief Elsie (3) and Wendy (4) are up to upstairs. (Sufficient unto the hour!) Yesterday, I gazed with a feeling of suppressed dismay as my husband poured treacle (molasses) onto his plate and proceeded to mop it up with bread. I ventured to remark: I shouldn't like to see the kiddies doing that! And he replied, "They can do it when they get old enough. As you know, we always do it this way in Canada." (I knew and recalled in my mind an incident when the twins and Freddie (2 years and 3 years old) had taken two packets of molasses upstairs and later had engaged in a pillow fight. There were feathers all over the landing, and what a time I had trying to sweep up sticky, downy feathers! And the children—well! Tar and feathers was a very close description! And I was far from amused.)

There was a Robin in the house. Yes, Gladys had an eye for the pretty and wonderful things in life, although struggling with the daily chores of washing, cleaning and getting all the children organised for school. 'The kids have gone back to school.' 'I polished the floor red.' 'The Carpenter finished his work.' 'I missed the Fishman (local shops drove 'round the outlying areas selling their ware).' 'Saw a butterfly.' 'Hark! Hark! The merry lark.'

(I always love to read these tiny notes Gladys included in her writing. I'll just include them as I go along.)

September 1953

Saturday 12 Sep '53 – I gazed in utter fascination at George's head. I couldn't get used to it. He'd had the top shaved at the barbers.

Sunday 13 Sep '53 – Took the eight children for a walk up to the hostel. George polished floors.

Monday 14 Sep '53 – The wool came – in spools!

Tuesday 15 Sep '53 – Rations.

Wednesday 16 Sep '53 – Fish and veg.

Thursday 17 Sep '53 – Chocolates. 10th Wedding Anniversary. The cake was O.K. Not the pie.

Saturday 19 Sep '53 – I went to town. Got dishes.

Monday 21 Sep '53 – Letter from Aunt Sarah.

Tuesday 22 Sep '53 – Feeding Evelyn on breast and bottle still.

Saturday 26 Sep '53 – George went to town. Got accumulator.

Monday 28 Sep '53 – Evelyn's head rather scruffy. Try olive oil.

Wednesday 30 Sep '53 – Rained heavily all day. Very stormy.

1954

January – March

I tried to do a sketch of myself as presently situated, but not having the Giles genius, my perspective got all out of focus. Myself at the washtub, with a huge pile of clothing and dishes piled at the sink. The baby is howling. Charlie, Elsie and Wendy are fighting. Freddie coming in soaking wet after sailing his boat in the burn. Kay and Linda are in difficulties with their knitting. Susan (6) 'has got nothing to play with' (later she cuts off Charlie's, Elsie's, and Wendy's hair). What sights!

Here is the original sketch Gladys made:

George stays in bed for breakfast, so that he 'won't be under my feet,' he says. The floor just has to be scrubbed in case we should have a visitor. Elsie (3) carefully tore out all the savings stamps! Dr. Walker is away on holiday in a cloth cap (or bunnet, Scottish name for a bonnet). There is a very cold wind. It's a holiday for the kids not sitting Qualifying [an examination at age 12. Now called a Merit Certificate]. We covered their NEW Books. (All school books were on loan from the school and had to be covered to keep them as presentable as possible. We mostly used brown paper or sometimes wallpaper.) The washing (laundry) was done by 10 a.m. I put up swings and a hammock for the kids. I made a garden at the back door and planted daffodils. Bought lettuce seeds from Muil and Fraser. It was dry today and not quite so cold. Wrote a letter to the Daily Express and Fairy Soap contest. (Gladys was a regular contributor to newspapers and magazines. I think she just loved writing, but the rewards were also a supplement to our income, which never seemed to stretch as far as the needs of a whole bunch of fast-growing Irving children! At this moment there were 8 children aged between 1 and 11.)

I edited ensuing snippets from each month. Don't forget that Gladys was now expecting baby number nine! It's amazing she even found time to keep a diary at all! Later on, her writing is more story-like.

April

I cleaned up the living room, then worked in the garden. It was a lovely day. The Doctor visited the four houses of the forestry cottages. Ours was number 2 of the forestry cottages, Alt-na-Blathaich, with the white car in front. Across the road is Loch Eck.

The forestry cottages and me in front of nr.2 recently

Charlie and Evelyn's chickenpox is healing. Enjoyed singing with the kiddies. Got nothing done. Wrote a letter to Brenda to ask my Dad (Grampy Morgan) if he wants the washing machine. George still has his beard. Grampy doesn't want the washing machine. Brenda is in hospital.

George hasn't got his beard now. Got trees for planting. School holidays are now on until the 16th of April. Went into town, then I got lost, then I fell. I bought 2 dozen eggs at 2/6 a dozen. Elsie stuck a crayon up her nose. So I sent for the doctor. He came and removed the crayon. George was on fire duty. Mrs Austin borrowed oil. We planted potatoes in the garden. I'm feeling awfully browned off these days for some reason. I honestly don't know why. Kids went back to school…. George says it's entirely my own fault I'm pregnant again. I don't understand.

I did some gardening and planted carrot seeds, also lettuce and radishes. Went to town with Kay. Got a woolly suit gift for Evelyn (I remember that suit! It was a warm, brown teddy onesie). Planted out daisies and parsley in the garden. Mrs Austin returned the oil she'd borrowed. She mentioned that she still has a Valor pricker (Whatever that is! Valor was a small paraffin heater), I had loaned her. She then borrowed a tin of dried milk (baby milk). I finished knitting the first sock. I did a washing. Took Charlie, Elsie and Wendy up into the woods to get primroses. Carried pails of water out to water the garden. Made the dinner. George hosed the garden and the windows. I started knitting the second sock. Saw McCallum (one of our neighbours) looking at our backyard for a full 10 minutes while I made the beds.

May

George went to town on the 1 p.m. bus. I planted out cabbage plants. Heavy rain. Evelyn is 9 months old. Wrote to Dr Walker and asked about inoculations. Washed the kids for their school Medical examination, but they didn't get their Medical. Letter from the school doctor to the dentist regarding Freddie's teeth. George says that Mrs Calder took sick today and has gone to the hospital. She isn't due with her baby for six weeks yet. The coal came. Pay him tomorrow. We got five bags of coal.

A letter came with 1st day Cover Malta Stamps, Malta Government. Washed my hair and went to town. Weather faired. Brought home two pairs of worn boots. George gave them to Austin (another one of our neighbours). Brought sand home with Freddie. The young neighbour-boy, Calum Austin, was on the road and stopped five private cars. My cold is still in my chest. Lovely morning. I heard a cuckoo; then I transplanted a few more plants. Never a minute's rest this day. I'm worn out.

Ice cream was 2/6. Remember to pay for the papers. I gave money to the Postman for them. The Doctor called on Mr Austin. He has a cold. My nasturtiums are coming up well, also the mint. I must get some lime for the garden this week and bonemeal as well. I have a sore spine-end.

Linda left her cardy (cardigan) at school. I told Kenneth Stewart that Freddie has to sit in the BACK of the car. A one-armed boy with a wooden case asked when there's a bus. I sent a letter (Exciting Stories) to the Sunday Post. Dull day today, close and rain-like. Kay couldn't find her coat or jacket. We got oil for the heater. Swept and swept the floor this morning. I rushed around, just finished washing the children, when the Doctor came. He vaccinated Susie and inoculated Evelyn, Charlie, Elsie and Wendy. Gave me my line for elastic stockings and Food Office Maternity Benefit. Mrs Austin got one tin of dried milk from the nurse. I went to town (Dunoon) and bought a pineapple (needed sugar). I wore my long brown skirt, short black jacket, black net gloves, black high heels, and new stockings. (Wow! Very fifties!) Paid for the coal.

It's a lovely, beautiful morning. I took the eight children for a walk down the shore of Loch Eck, about 1½ miles away. They played in the sand and paddled. Evy enjoyed it very much, and it was warm. I did a washing. Sent a letter regarding the washing machine. I'm feeling played out. Messed around in the garden all morning. Transplanted lettuce. Nurse Morgan brought orange juice. Mrs Austin won potatoes. I gave Mrs Craig (also one of our neighbours) a milk card. Breakfast today was cornflakes, scrambled egg and sliced sausage for the kiddies. Kay chattered incessantly till she nearly missed the bus. Think I owe Mr Moore for oil. George went up for Jimmy's horse so that Angus could take it to the smiddy (Farrier). I spotted a swallow hovering in front of the window this morning, then cleaned up the backyard. Evelyn is awfully fussy. It's her second front tooth. Paid Mr Moore for the oil.

Coal came, and I got two bags for 11/3. Paid also for the last load. Altogether 39/4 ½, all clear with coal. The doctor was at Austin's; she had finally put 15-month-old Morag in the playpen. I gave a tinker some tea. The Golligwog brooch came, and the new ration books too. Mr Calder handed in tomatoes! George says they have sent Mrs Calder back to Glasgow Hospital. The weather is dull and there's an icy wind. Mr Austin borrowed 1 oz tobacco and ½lb margarine. Mrs Austin borrowed library books. Heavy rains all day. Mrs Austin went to town but didn't pay back the margarine and tobacco as she'd promised. My margarine is low, and so is bread. I went fishing. Caught nothing. Only four pints of milk. (Ha, ha! Was the milk swimming in the loch?)

I have all the ration books. And five pints of milk. I think about the diet. George thinks about his holidays. I made lentil soup for dinner on Wednesday. The weather is too close and hot. I'm breathless and useless. Posted three letters. I got the washing (laundry) done by 10 a.m., then raked the potato patch till midday. Dinner was potatoes, carrots and meat. Still warm outside, but a cooler breeze. Finished knitting George's socks.

June

It promises to be a warm day. I heard a cuckoo. The kids went back to school this morning. Freddie got a cold while swimming in the loch. The oil has not been paid yet. I'm practicing my diet. No bread at all. Charlie has a narrow shave with a car—Wheww! I must keep the lock on the gate.

After a week on Energen rolls (no diet except to cut out bread and sugar and potatoes), I find I've lost 2 lbs. Bought diet food. Start my diet in earnest today. Sunday night, I'm very hungry but no pains. Second liquid day. Confess to a slight hunger. Told Freddie to bring home Energen rolls. At last, proteins! But I've got an awful head cold. Runny nose and sneezing my head off all day. The Grocer Coop (the Cooperative delivery van) wants their bill cleared – Oh dear!

Feeling exhausted with my cold and getting the kids half-decent looking for school. The clothing van came. Ran my bill up to 30/-. Evelyn howls and howls. I bought shoes from McFadyen. My teeth need attention. They're giving me neuralgia. My cold isn't quite so bad. I'm feeling bad-tempered this morning between the irritation of the midges and everything else.

(Midges are a tiny mosquito-type of flying insects. They come in clouds and bite you—very annoying! Sometimes midges or midgies are called gnats, though the US English 'no-see-ums' is much more colourful and also accurate. Make no mistake, when the conditions are right, these wee beasties can be an awful irritation. Check out the Kenneth McKellar YouTube version of his song and the lyrics on <u>Kenneth McKellar - The Midges Lyrics | Lyrics.com</u> – "With teeth like piranhas they drive ye bananas." And very appropriate: "Now never forget, when the sun's going to set, And the midges arise on **Loch Eck**.")

On 5 August, Evelyn goes on dried milk. Dr Walker gave the final Diphtheria inoculations to Wendy, Elsie, Charlie and Evelyn. He will be back on the 9th of July. The midges are bad. I did a big washing (laundry).

Wheeeeeuw! What a morning of bathing and dressing all 8 of the children (ages 1 – 9). But had them all ready AND myself too, when Mr Jackson arrived in the Forestry van to take us to the school sports day being held in Benmore Gardens. They had decorated the driveway into the grounds with huge trees (the so-called "Avenue of Giant Redwoods," with the tallest giant sequoia of Europe), and masses of flowering rhododendrons. We walked past flowering shrubs to the expansive lawn in front of a large, turreted house. The sun shone, the midges sang—Midges! Oh, the bane of my life every summer. The baby was good. She had a sleep wrapped in my heavy coat. The children ran races and enjoyed ice cream, lemonade and a bag of buns. I nursed Evelyn when she woke up and exchanged a few words with people. Soon it was time to get home, and Mr Jackson packed all the Loch Eck kiddies back into his van and drove us home. George and 2-year-old Charlie hadn't got back from town. I had to boil water to wash the dinner dishes and then made the beds. Eventually, George and Charlie came home. I got the children all to bed and was certainly ready for my own bed by the time it was 10 p.m. But oh, those midgie bites!

Benmore Gardens the Giant Redwoods
Photo Courtesy of Sybil Gray at Benmore Gardens.

Midges are bad again. I used half the bottle of anti-midge on my legs, which are badly bitten. I transplanted Brussels sprouts. Mrs Calder had a baby girl. I'll try Oil of Citronella for repelling the midges. Used up all the camphorated oil in an effort to discourage the midges. Did the washing. The rain threatens but holds off; then it rained all night.

Still raining. Evelyn is getting more confidence and takes an occasional one-step. I feel I am losing a little weight, and actually, I am feeling more fit to cope with work. I think I'd like to call my new baby 'June Rose' if she's a girl; if a boy, John Henry will do. George brought home a good spring bed and mattress. (A shrill scream rent the air. I had opened the matchbox containing my son's pet beetle!) Halfway through my diet! Received a letter this morning from Mrs Bruce, who is inquiring about McGowan. She saw my name and address in the Sunday Mail. I went to town. George killed 12 rats at the barn. Got a parcel of stuff from town. It rained all day. My washing is still hanging outside and has been there since Friday. Midges are bad.

Nancy (the horse) is lame. They sent George down to the barn. I sent the postcard of Loch Eck to Grampy Morgan. Mr Austin gave George 6 worn shirts and collars and Freddie a pullover. Evelyn takes 1, 2, and 3 steps alone. She is 10½ months. Only 3 teeth. Fruit day, today and tomorrow, that's my diet. We received a postcard from Grampy Morgan saying Brenda is in Gogarburn Institution after nine weeks in hospital and two weeks at home. I asked the fishmonger if he was feeling all right. He didn't look at all well. Apparently, he got a soaking yesterday. I saw Mr Austin come home on his bike. He says he's on two days' holiday. High wind and showers. Evelyn is very fussy, so I gave her a powder. George came home at 2.30 p.m. saying Nancy (the horse) can't work anymore. Mrs Austin says Dr Walker is calling on her today to see Mr Austin's throat. It's pouring rain and George went away up with his bike on the Forestry track. I'm making junket and treacle toffee, keeping four wee ones in order (I hope) and trying to finish knitting my scarf.

Tiresome, wet day. Wendy is still bilious. I put Evelyn out to sleep in the rain. Bathed the twins and Freddie for tomorrow. It's the last day of my diet. I got up at 4.45 a.m. to get the twins and Freddie dressed and ready to go to Edinburgh. George took Nancy up to Whistlefield while he cut the grass up at Stuart's today. Wendy has still got stomach 'flu and Evelyn is walking everywhere! At 10 months! The weather is dry but with a chilly wind, then warmer with the sun. I did a washing. George started his holidays by cycling to Dunoon and going to the pictures (movies). I'm not doing so well with my diet. Had to eat potatoes and bread with gravy, as there was nothing else.

George took Charlie into Dunoon. The boy at the store gave Wendy comics. We slept in! Till 10 to 8. What a rush. I took Wendy and Elsie to the school closing. They enjoyed it very much! The four children at school all received prizes.

July

George went to town. It's still raining. George, Susie and Charlie went up to Whistlefield to see Mrs Ina Bennett, who gave them 6d each. Got a letter from Grampy Morgan. Brenda is happy and content in Gogarburn. George went on a cycle run and I did a big washing. Two heavy rain showers. There's a cold wind. Evelyn is 11 months old. Horribly midgy this morning. George and Susie went away to town for money this morning. I didn't sleep well and felt tired. Evelyn is well on with her walking and gets into all sorts of mischief.

Much nicer day. Cold in the morning and windy. I washed 6 big blankets and 2 small ones. George put them through the wringer. I cleaned up the backyard. Weeded my gardens and washed out the pram. Polished the front porch and bathroom. Put the clean, dry blankets back on the beds. Put away clothes off the pulley and hung up infants' clothes, which I had laid in the cupboard and they smelled damp. I had cramps all night. Received Canadian comics with the post. I'm not well. Got gastric flu, I think, with cramps. Took brandy and sherry and dry toast. Feeling slightly better. George weighs 14 stone, 4lbs (and is slim as a rake!). He went to town in the morning and got a few spare parts for the bicycle he's fixing. I quarrelled with George last night. I did send the half-pint bottle down. Some sun but it is cold today. No coal. No money for the Store—there's a new Storeboy. Dash! They've not delivered the meat I ordered!

Laura Jane will be the name unless I change my mind again.

Except, of course, it be a boy, then Henry John will be my joy!

Today I bought 1 lb apples from Tweedley, that's 4 for 1/8 or 5d each! And one was rotten! I went to the dentist. He did two soft fillings and one hard one. He's not sure about the back tooth. It may have to come out on 6th August. I did shopping till 5.30 p.m. Weighed myself with my heavy coat, which weighs 7 lbs. I was 13 stone 8lbs. That means 13stone 1lb without the coat. I put on my slacks(!) and went up to the woods to collect wood. Got honeysuckle and planted it, as well as a rowan tree. Also, got one piece of rotten wood. Had difficulty getting Freddy to go for wood. I went to town. My weight is still the same. Very close today. We owe Mr McDougall 13/6 for a battery (Jenkin), and also for 2 tubes and a tyre for the bicycle.

I did a big washing. The kids went for a walk. A man took their photo. Then I did a small washing. I made rice pudding into curried rice. They ate it! Evelyn got soaked in her pram by a heavy rain shower when I forgot to put up the hood. Dr Walker came at 4 p.m. He'll be back in four weeks, on 26 August. I turned up Wendy's dress and sewed it, then repaired Linda's coat and sewed 8 buttons onto Wendy's coat, then I mended the sleeve and darned one sock. I am tired, and the kids are fed up with the rain. The baker said he would get me a gramophone. George was up at the bothy (a basic shelter, usually left unlocked and available for anyone to use free of charge) all day, doing nothing, but he never said one word of what gossip I'll bet they did have. Freddie told me a long yarn about Mr Austin's misdeeds! Evelyn is playing with a canful of buttons. The girls were awfully pleased with themselves and very secretive about their good deed while they insisted I go up to make my bed. I had to be terribly pleased to find that they had made it for me!

George went to town where he got the £2 Postal Order and paid 3/3 for our newspapers. Also snaps, which were quite good. The parcel came—two really good blankets and a good coat for Freddie. I went on Freddie's bike, but didn't do much else today. Still cold weather. Wrote some letters, one to Mum (that's Grandma Irving in Canada) with snaps. I posted the letter to Grandma and one to the Food Office in Glasgow. Sent Freddie for oil. We have no coal and very little wood. It rained the whole afternoon. I did the washing and hoped to hang it out today. There was a small rainbow over the loch. I've no money for the store today, and this is rent week. Rain. Rain. Rain. I went to collect wood and sawed some of it.

It's a better day. I sawed wood and swept thoroughly downstairs. The McLarens moved out. Rent is off this week (Wilkinson).

Wow! I've won £5 in a Daily Express 'Wet Weather' contest! I went to town. Had a look at an old (50-year-old, I think) Singer Sewing Machine and bought a mincer.

August

Mrs Austin hasn't returned the tea. There's a high wind, and it's warmer today. Tidied up and did washing. The mince I'd bought and pre-cooked on Saturday has gone a bit "off." However, I washed it and did it up with onions and tomato soup and they all ate it (I didn't). I've ordered 10 pan loaves (bread - see Pan loaf on Wikipedia) from the store for next Monday. Posted three letters to the Sunday Mail, then started knitting a baby's vest (blue wool is all I've got). So, George wants to know what I'm saving. What does he think we live on? Just wait till I give him his grocery and butcher's bills! (Says he was kidding me!) Mr Austin borrows a tin of dried milk. I sent Freddie for oil. Mr Austin saw him and added his can to Freddie's load. Awfully midgy today. Evelyn's birthday (1 year). Mrs Austin paid back the dried milk, but not the tea. George paid McDougall and Muil and Fraser. I did the washing. It poured with rain all day.

Sent money to Mr Moore by Freddie. So that should be the oil clear. I went to the dentist today. It was still raining, and I had to stand nearly all the way on the bus there and back. Gosh, was I ever sore, physically. The kids got the bread (and cakes!) and paid for them. It's a fine morning. George wants to buy the sewing machine when he goes to town today. Evelyn (unnoticed) takes the dish of butter off the table, the dish of sugar, and a spoon. Has a sup and handful from each dish. George paid £1 down on an old sewing machine. I have stopped the Sunday papers. At night, it intrigued me to see a light steady on the ceiling. I looked out and saw a man with the stable lamp saying to a woman and man: "Well, you are not going to wander around here." We get 6 pints of milk starting from today. Milk now costs 8/- a week.

We have ordered 10 pan loaves (bread) to come today with the Store van. It came. It was drier this morning. Did a washing. I took Evelyn and the others a walk as far as George's work. Nancy (the horse) lost a shoe. George hurt his big toe. The weather was fine and dry. I gave David Tweedley my letter to post to Mrs B. McNaughton, Glendorsal (shareholder in the Scottish Daily Express), about my letter winning £5, which I didn't get YET.

It's a better day today with warm sunshine. George took the last lettuce out. Evelyn is singing and clapping her hands. No mail arrived except snaps from Boots. I will send them to Grampy Morgan and Mrs Gilmour. Well! The cheque for £5 in payment for my published letter has arrived. Verrry nice too. I'm quite thrilled though I did worry because it took it two weeks to come through. George cycled to town. Freddie paid 8/4 for oil and said a man gave him 2/- and an orange and candy on the bus. The Fishman wants to cash my cheque. I wonder what the Daily Express said to Mrs McNaughton when she phoned! I posted three letters—one to Grampy, one to Mrs Gilmour and one an order for clothing.

Mince and potatoes for dinner. I did the washing. Sent off 6/6 for papers and my competition entry for 'Men only.' A birthday card arrived for George from Frank Caldwell. Rain all afternoon. Rather cold. I received an invoice for the parcels. I refused to give Mrs Austin dried milk. She is a nuisance. Freddie kindled the fire. I've no coal. How can I earn money to help clear debts? I fixed up things for school starting. Wendy starts school today. She's pretty well dressed (with new shoes!) That's five off to school and three at home. A letter arrived from Grampy. I wrote back: "I must say that it seems unusual for Aunt Sarah and Kate Savers to be so pally with Brenda just since she went to Gogarburn, seeing as how they never replied to the letters I sent asking them to be your housekeeper or help in the house since we were leaving." Still no parcel we're waiting for. It's a lovely day. The midgies are biting. I had a bath. Bought work boots for George.

I'm expecting the Doctor today. It's very drizzly weather. The Cowal Highland Games are on. I burnt my hand with hot fat. Oh, what a long day. George went to the pictures (movies). It rained, but I went for a walk. George has a few days' holiday. He went to see the coal office about the overcharge. They insist that I have made a mistake. Back in March, too. In future we get receipts for coal. George lifted the potato crop and I helped a bit. We got nearly three bags. My burnt hand is still a nuisance. The wind dropped and the midges were bad. Used 2 gallons of oil to date (one week).

September

Did a good cleanup. We bought three cups from Gavin Scott. The Jehovah's Witness man, Mr Scoley, called. We studied the brochure: 'New Heavens and New Earth.' George bought pork chops in town, then later chopped wood for the fire. I did the washing and wrote three letters to newspapers (competitions). Susan and Wendy have Miss Hall as their teacher. Mr Moore delivered oil.

The parcel I'm expecting still hasn't arrived. I bought bread: 4 pans, 2 brown, 1 dozen rolls and a ½ lb biscuits. He was going to charge me as well for bread and rolls Austin got yesterday. Told the butcher they have charged me for the bacon I didn't get last week. The bread delivery came (6 pans, 4 plain and 1 packet of rich tea biscuits). Mr Moore delivered the oil—he says he'll send the bill. I thought it had been cleared! I bought leeks, a packet of Manilla envelopes and writing paper, baby ribbon and wool, margarine and dripping (cooking fat). We received the invoice for Susie's shoes.

Went to a meeting on Sunday. It's my birthday today, 38 years old. Mrs Simmonds asked for Dettol. George brought home a bottle of cider. I wanted earrings. Tried to get a day off duty. George prepared the dinner after I asked him, but I still had to do all the rest. I took a bath and noticed my varicose veins; it makes me sick to look at them. Nearly three months yet before the baby is due, too. I finished knitting the baby's white vest! It's Elsie's birthday, she's 4 years old. I bought a melon. We got deer meat (venison). I sent in an application for Welfare Milk. Kept Kay off school. George has hurt his leg and has a sore back. I bought one yard of winceyette for 3/6. George speaks of a pressure lamp he's buying. Kay is off school with a cough. It is very frosty this morning, with sunshine. Evie got a skinned nose. I gave the children their school dinner money. Dry weather today. The Doctor was at Austin's. The Veterinary got a horse. I gave Freddie money for tickets for Kay's dinners. She wants to go back to school today. Charlie has a sore ear and a cold. We sold 1 gallon of oil to Mrs Austin. Received milk tokens, etc., from the Food Office.

George starts his new compartment. Charlie is a bit better. It's very wet.

October

I gave Freddy money for oil and his bus fare, as well as money to give to Mrs Stuart to pay for the papers and money for school dinners. Wrote a letter to the Forestry Commission for a telephone. Not sure if I've done right in doing it off my own bat. Dr Walker arrived at about 6 p.m. Got the family allowance form signed. The coal came about 1 p.m. I sent for oil (and got a receipt). George says, Nancy, the horse cannot work any longer. She's going to the "Nackery" (to be put down). The slippers I'd ordered came. I put fur on them. George drew 2 weeks' Family Allowance in town. He brought home fish, meat, milk, and the papers.

George went to Stirling for hay. It rained heavily all day. Nevertheless, I did a washing and hung it out, then made soup. No papers came today. I was sick and restless all night. Thought the baby was going to arrive. Couldn't eat or knit or do anything all day. It's Wendy's birthday (5). Kept Susie home. Then next day kept Linda home to help, but, like with Susie, I have to keep at her all the time to get a job done. This is exhausting in itself. Got cold cramps in my tum-tum. The following day, I kept Kay off school to help (!)

Help(!). Still, they are young, but they'll have to learn. An old tinker (or traveller) woman was at the door. "Nothing", says I."

She says, "I'm looking for an old pram but I see you've a baby in it."

"Aye, I've got too many babies," I laughed.

"Oh, ye can't have too many, hen," says she. With which profound remark, she departed. (The word "hen" is a Scottish colloquial word of endearment for a woman or girl.) Later, Mrs McCallum said that the woman's name was Cameron and that she'd been on the road for three years at least. "She's got two big rings on her fingers," says I.

"Oh, she's always covered in rings," says Mrs McCallum.

Mr Scoley meets Mr Irving. Freddie is off school today to do the housework. But I'm feeling a bit better and hope to be as usual next week. Worked hard in the morning and did all the upstairs and wiped down the stairs. Made Kay, Linda and Susie do a bit of work downstairs. My-oh-my! Slippers split at the side, so I returned them. Postage was 10d - (it's getting dear with postage!). George bought an oil cloth and hair-clippers. Mr McCallum gets Doctor Walker in. Got George to fix the stairs and help with some shifting around. He mended a chair. We received a letter from Mrs Gilmour, Ontario, Canada. I wrote a letter to Grampy Morgan and posted two letters (one to the papers and one to Woman Magazine). Hung the washing out in the rain. Made soup. The kids are on holiday till next

Wednesday. We got three bags of coal, delivered by three men in a large red truck, registration KGD 707.

George got the stove fixings in town; then he worked up at the barn for a while. Got a letter from Grampy saying Brenda is happy and comfortable, and he is quite content himself. He is due to retire in a year's time. Fine, cold, frosty, sunny and dry day. The kids are still on holiday and playing up at the quarry. We got one gallon of oil, brought home by Freddie, who was offered a lift in a police car. Freddie hauled logs, helped by Johnnie. I gave them 6d each. Johnnie refused, so I told Freddy to buy sweets and share them. Very raw and cold. Bathed eight kids, all fitted out with eight clean vests.

Feel slightly in the dumps, but relieved to see five kids off to school. I've clouted Elsie the whole morning for girning when I'm busy. I paid Mr Moore for the oil we got on Wednesday. Also bought bread, but he still owes me three halves. The kids (five of them) got all dressed up for the Halloween party. George went as well and quite enjoyed it. They all came home at 11 p.m. with a few cakes and nuts.

November

Monday morning. At 9.05 a.m., and do I ever feel a wreck after dealing with the kids. Finding clothes that aren't too ragged or dirty is no easy job. Socks and shoes are a problem. Then they've (as usual) lost their pencils, their boots, their bags and I don't know what else. I can find one glove, no hankies, lost the hairbrush. Got one book between Elsie and Charlie. Oh, well. Monday morning generally is the worst! Thought I was heading for the terror of the torture rack last night (the labour ward), but relieved to find I was mistaken. George says: "Why the worry? You know all about it!" That's just the trouble—I know only too well what I'm in for. (But I'll try not to think about it.)

It's 9.30 a.m. now. What a relief to get them all out of the house so I can sit down for 5 minutes and enjoy the quietness. I gave Freddie money for a book of dinner tickets. The papers still have to be paid for last week. Evelyn had a fall. Bought shoes, a nightdress, two pairs of knickers, men's socks, children's socks, wool and a vest from McFadyen. Bought stockings from another traveller. Then I bought beetroot, fish and sprouts from Tweedley and sent for oil.

I expect Dr Walker today, so I've to get the place cleaned and tidied now. He came at 4.30 p.m. That's fine, says he after taking my blood pressure (all the kids were in). Next to the other room for examination. Baby's position is fine. Head well down and the baby is the right way up.

"Yes, just one," says the doctor, and he's coming back in three weeks' time. (My oh my, time is running in). I'm now planning my campaign of the birth. I will be calm when I get the first pain or sign. I shall suffer in silence (at least as silently as I can). Then, I'll get dressed for the journey (after notifying the persons to be notified). I'll get my soap, towel, toothbrush and all necessities for a week in the hospital (I am at the moment having slight pains and strains, but I think it is possibly because of constipation). Then I'll drink a cup of my hot tea and wait patiently for the conveyance to the hospital. (I hope it's a daytime job this time.) I shall endeavour not to fear the pains but to meet them halfway and relax as much as possible. Endurance and courage. I shall say to myself—Endure. Endure, have Courage!

I had an argument with George. This followed my report of Freddy with the Stewarts as annoying Mr McCallum, who looked fit to kill Freddie when he came to the door. He was white with vindictive rage—and oh! The look he gave Freddie at the door! My oh my! I don't think I can feel quite so friendly to the McCallums after that AWFUL look…

Eh, dearie me, ah feel like an auld wifie the day! Got a drill in the muscles of my bottom and can hardly walk around, and sitting is uncomfortable. George went to town and got two weeks' Family Allowance. He bought dry goods, including rubber sheeting and foodstuffs. I was keen on getting a dolly to dress as a gift for Evelyn, but George had no money left, so I felt disappointed. However, he promised to get it next time. Knitted part of a sock. Heavy frost on the ground.

Brought in the nappies (diapers) from the washing line. I decided to try to whiten them by boiling and then I went upstairs. The pot boiled over on pressure and the oil started blazing. Came downstairs with a handful of wet sheets. Elsie was yelling. I threw the sheets over the stove after lifting off the pot. Oh, WHAT a mess! And gas escaping after I got the flames quenched. I had to put the thing outside to cool off and get rid of the gas. I had no paper or sticks to start the Rayburn. Finally, got it going by 3 p.m., then I got dinner prepared. I'm feeling terribly played out. George came in and gave Freddie an awful belting. He had been tormenting Catherine McCallum (at the instigation of the Stewarts, I bet). I was quite upset, and it wasn't helping me any. My slippers came today (size 5). Sent a letter to "Woman Magazine" (Susan's hair).

The Storeman gave me a nice soup bone. Muil and Fraser gave us a small spice loaf. We were ordered to keep the kids in the yard away from the Stewarts. Mrs Stewart told me they'd never heard anything about the McCallums cart! I was surprised. She said none of the school kids speak to Catherine McCallum. In fact, Miss Henderson told her she'd have to stop her nonsense as she'd been crying because 5-year-old Sandy had hit her. It surprised me to see Mrs McCallum avoid me at the Fishman's van.

More rain and wind. I'm feeling the strain of being pregnant. The baby seems to be putting on weight fast—I'm SO TIRED— Sent Freddie to town for George's tobacco and bike bulb. He saw Mr Scoley and went round with him. Mrs Austin borrowed an envelope. Mr Austin borrowed cigarette papers.

Frosty and sunny day today. George dug a bit of the front lawn. He gave McCallum and Austin books back. I bathed six of the children.

Just don't know how I got through this morning, for my legs were sore, and I was breathless, too. However, I coped with breakfast somehow, but getting clean clothes for the girls to start school this morning, well! The clothes position is hopeless. Their dresses are done. They have one pair of socks each at present. Their knickers – Susie and Kay need a new pair. As for shoes! Charlie, Elsie and Evelyn could do with new footwear (when Elsie's done chattering to me, I'll continue). Well, it is a struggle. Last night, I felt slight (false) pains, but they were probably caused by constipation. I'm feeling very restless, so I suppose as soon as the actual pains start, all my nerves and muscles will tense right up. I think I've got most of the stuff necessary for going to the hospital.

Utter exasperation has made me exhausted this morning. I used my hand and the belt, of course. Evelyn nearly had the pot of boiling porridge over her, and then she grabbed the oil lamp. Then I gave Mrs Stewart money for 1lb margarine as Muil and Fraser isn't coming today. I didn't have a good night's rest last night either. Fine dry day, but cold and sunny. Freddie took 2 tins to school for leftovers.

Keen frost, then thick, damp fog—it's very cold. My 'sciatica' is bothering me yet. My tummy looks lowered. It won't be long now, I shouldn't think. When I get the first pain, I shall just say to myself, "I'm glad the wait is over." My movements are awkward, and it is difficult to get a good night's rest. The coal is nearly finished and there isn't much wood.

George is digging drains in the mud. We got a surprise from Gavin Scott today. They gave us a big parcel of clothes, mostly fitting Charlie, but all except Evelyn and George shared in. There was even a sideboard runner. I felt pleased because most of it was in good order.

Well, we've done pretty well this fortnight, burning two fires even up till today when the coalman came. He was tuppence short as he didn't have enough change. I must get oil today too. I'm feeling much more active today than I've felt during the last two days. So, I'd better be careful not to push ahead too much though I would like to get a good washing done.

Freddy got tobacco for George and spent 2/6 on himself plus 1/- on his bus fare. Rates at £7 odds came. George had to go into town for the Family Allowance so I can pay some bills. George has a toothache. He went up to Jenkins (and bought a radio!)

George went into town and got 2 back teeth out. Then went back to work. The boss told him he's getting a horse and to prepare the barn for another two horses. Mr McCallum is getting one, then there is Mr Calder's horse, Jean, which is to go in the barn as well and receive treatment for her sore leg. Johnnie Stewart has measles. Kept Freddie home. I have a few shillings kept aside for dinner tickets. Kept Freddie home. Susie fell through the ceiling into the bathroom. Johnnie does not have measles. I washed my hair.

I kept Susie home. She cut her finger badly. It was a dry and cold day today. I did all the washing and hung it out. Mrs Stewart didn't come over. Her husband has flu. Mr Calder was going for hot water for Jean (his horse). George's herb tobacco and Susan's medicine arrived. I washed and had a bath. The Doctor came at 3.30 pm. He mentioned iron tablets. He said he'd be back in two weeks, maybe. I gave Evy a golliwog I'd made. The pressure lamp came. I tidied up, but Mr Scoley didn't come. The Nurse called. We got six bottles of cod liver oil. Mr Scoley came to the door for a minute. George got his new horse and said goodbye to Nancy.

Freddie went to town in the morning and spent the whole time by the store. He came home hungry but denounced the dinner as horrid. Contrarily he intended eating it in the living room, but I made him take all his table setting out of here. Next, he smashed the precious jar of jam. After being scolded, he removed the mess with the shovel. I sent him for coal. The dross is all stuck to the shovel with the jam. It falls on the hearth, then he sweeps the sticky mess with the fender brush, messing up the brush and the hearth. I nearly explode. When he's done complaining about nothing to do, I set him to washing the dishes. He finished that job and yells for a towel and snatches Kay's drying towel out of her hand and smashes a big white plate to the floor. Again, I am very angry. The next mess is made by Kay who brings in the Syrup of Figs (Susie had complained for half an hour about a sore tummy) and drips it all over the floor. I made her wipe it up. But every time I walk over the living room floor my feet stick and my shoes stick in the kitchen too (oh—what's the use?). Then I see Lux-flakes all over the kitchen floor and discover Freddie has used nearly a whole large packet of Lux to wash a few dishes. If I let myself get mad, I get all breathless and my heart thumps, so I try hard not to say too much, though I'm very angry indeed. (And, oh, the mess the kitchen is in after they leave it !) But I'm not able to cope, so I leave it all, and that isn't the half of it. But let's draw a curtain over it and go read a book.

Not feeling well at all. George pays £3 for a radio.

Ah'm No weel. (Scots way of saying "I'm not well.") Mr Austin borrows a ½ oz of tobacco—promises it back for tomorrow.

Feeling a bit better today, must have had the 'flu. I'm craving an orange. Mr Austin didn't return the tobacco today as promised. George put an aerial up in the attic.

December

The clothing man called. He brought the nightdress which I had to fix at the neck. I hope it wears well. He will be back in 3 weeks' time (just before Christmas, he said). The Fishman came. He gave Charlie an apple. Mrs Austin brought over a few wee dresses. (Evelyn has cut one into ribbons now). Then she sent over for 1lb marge. Then later she borrowed a book, "Silver Rock," and brought over 3 or 4 pairs of pants for Charlie. I hate accepting anything from her, but I don't know how to refuse without giving offence. Posted three Christmas cards to Canada.

I got methylated spirits and Susie's torch from the shop. A letter arrived from Grampy Morgan to say Aunt Mary was dead and cremated. George has Donald (his new horse) out. Stormy weather.

What a wind last night! Freddie went to town. Evy has a slight cough and a cold. George sawed wood. Mr Austin took out Paddy. I felt pretty bad but could do nothing. Thought my pains would start any minute. Mrs Stewart called and stayed to tidy up the place a bit. I paid for the school dinner tickets. Received a parcel from Mrs Gilmour. Mrs Austin brought in library books for an exchange.

Mrs Stewart called this morning to tidy up. I'm feeling fairly fine. The weather is milder. Mr Scoley called in. I'm dated today for the hospital. Freddie went to town. George got wood. Mrs Austin has Smoky (a cat maybe?). Tweedley didn't come today.

George sawed wood. I washed my hair. The chimney went on fire. I'm still here. It's slightly frosty and cold. I refused Mrs Stewart's offer of help today. Got 4 gallons oil. The coal is almost finished. I had to push Freddie out the door this morning to catch the school bus. I wonder WHEN? It rained all day. What a long day it's been. Susie was to stay home. Then just at bus time Freddie complained of being ill, so then there were two of them home. They just became more of a nuisance than a help with their carry on. Otherwise, I feel fairly fit. Mrs Stewart called. I'm feeling fine. So well in fact that I'm wondering if it's going to take another month??

I kept none of the school kids home today. I need a rest. Woman's paper says my date is scheduled for next Wednesday. Bought a cup, Brillo and prickers from Gavin Scott. I parcelled gifts for Grampy and Brenda. Freddie has a cough.

At 5.00-7.45 this morning, I had slight cramps with much discomfort. Uneasy. Got George to take the morning off. I just can't be definite, so won't go. Still feeling very uneasy. Sent the parcel to Grampy and Brenda. Very stormy weather.

A quiet night for me, and George and Evelyn slept pretty well. Very high gales with rain. Freddie is still at home. George went out to work. I didn't feel quite so bad today. Started on the Christmas pudding. Dr Walker called about 3.30 p.m. I didn't expect him. He told me I needed a course of iron tonic. But he never gave me a prescription for it. The examination showed everything to be in order. He thinks I'll be in hospital around the 24th of the month now. I am feeling rather tired from the strain.

Snow showers. The school party is today. George puts up the Christmas tree. The house looks Christmassy with decorations. Received a parcel and letter from Grandma (in Canada). Freddy received a Christmas card from Joy and Molly Jenkins. But we wonder WHAT is in the parcel? I gave money to Freddie for going into town. We hear there is to be a rise in the pay packet. I seem to have something to do and I can't think what it is!

Sunday 26 Dec '54

Dorothy Janet arrived at 4.15 a.m. She weighed 9½ lbs.

1955 January

The kids came home early because of snow.

Elsie, Freddy and Charlie in the front garden. A young neighbour in the cartie.
You can see Loch Eck across the road.

I dressed the wee ones and put them outside. Six times. More snow fell. I put curlers in. It's Charlie's birthday—he's 3 years old. Slight thaw and frost. Twins' birthday—they are now 8 years old. Three wee ones were fighting all morning. Linda and Freddie went to town. I collected the Family Allowance in Dunoon. The Nurse called. The pram arrived, no charge. I posted a card from Freddie to Grampy. I smashed one of our 2 cups, then broke a jar in the sink.

(From a letter to the Daily Express: I am sure these children don't see any sense in spending money on armaments to save their country and living conditions they haven't got. Some people would say: Oh, but this is a necessary evil, you get it in all countries. But I say, is evil necessary?)

I posted the letter to the Daily Express. Mrs Austin borrowed a tin of dried milk. I asked Cathie why Mrs Austin wanted the Doctor. Mrs Marshall called. We got a receipt for the Rates. I did a washing. Feeling washed out myself.

February

Mrs McFadyen sent a parcel of clothes. The Nurse called. Dorothy Janet weighs 11½ lbs. I told Mr Scoley no Bible study this week. Next week is his Assembly. Dr Walker called in to say he'd see me next week sometime. I did a washing. Elsie smashed a bottle of cod liver oil. Wendy spilled a packet of milk. Kay spilt the sugar bowl. I made the beds, served the dinner, darned socks, washed dishes, nursed the baby, etc.

Freddie went to Sunday School at Benmore. He helped George saw wood. Dr Walker persuaded me that sterilisation was too drastic a measure. (After having 9 children? Gladys told me that she'd been to the doctor and asked him whether anything could be done to not have any more babies. The doctor just shook his head and said, "Ach, missus, it's only the ninth child!" Well, thinks Gladys to herself, I wonder how he'd like having the next one!)

The kids are on holiday till Tuesday. The rent increase letter came. George brought home a gramophone.

Monday 21 Feb '55

George says, "Clear off debts, buy kids' shoes and save money for a flitting. We're getting out of here." Personally, I'll be pleased, for I'm never happy about that road. The kids are out on it too often and the traffic comes too fast round the corners.

March

We got 2 dresses from Mrs Stewart. Received a letter from Grampy Morgan. Brenda is getting false teeth. Freddie is off school. George sent a letter about a farm job. Kay and Freddie have temperatures (flu and bronchitis). Dr Walker said, "Bed for them."

Went to town. Got paints for Freddie and shoes for Susie and a blue hair ribbon. The Doctor came. Freddie is to stay in bed. I sent off three letters to the 'Scottish Farmer'. It's funny, but ever since we came here, I'd always wanted to get away. But things got in such a way – with all the extra work and odd debts, that I just can't see my way clear to be easy in my mind about a flitting. However, I guess I'll just have to make up my mind to make the desperate effort. So I have been writing and have four letters ready for the post.

April

Lovely day, sunny with a cool wind. A letter came from Peebles about a job. George went into town. Put an advert in the Scottish Farmer. We gave the Austin's the big oil-stove. George went to the Whist Drive, also to town. Donald (the horse) broke the fence. Received a letter from Mrs Gilmour. The kids are on holiday till the

19th of April. I planted peas and beets. Sent a letter to Nurse Morgan with Milk Tokens.

May

Received a letter from Glen Lyon, Perthshire, and sent a reply. The painters finished up. Went to town with Susie and Wendy. My thumb is very sore.

Mr Moore's car broke down. We received a letter from Perthshire saying that the job has been filled. Sent a letter to Dr Walker regarding my sore thumb. The weather is still very cold with hailstones. We have no coal. The clothier called, but I didn't buy anything. Dr Walker called. George got a letter from the Glasgow Corporation Water Department about needing a worker for Loch Katrine. George left on his bike for an interview in Glasgow for the Loch Katrine job. There is a rail strike on. We received a telegram from Glen Lyon. The farmer, Mr D. McNiven, is coming on Sunday!

June

Mrs Austin is sick today. I guess it's the 'flu that's going around. Dorothy has a bad throat. It's all arranged that we go to Glen Lyon on Monday 13th June. I sent letters to the schoolteacher, Grampy, Nurse Morgan and Dr Walker. Also to my mother-in-law, Mrs Irving and Mrs Gilmour in Canada. George says his boss knew last Thursday that we were leaving? Who told? Lost Wendy's schoolbook. George brought home a chain.

Monday 13 June '55

We flitted (moved) to Bondhu Cottage, Glen Lyon, nearby Aberfeldy in the Scottish Highlands.

Bondhu Cottage

Carnban Castle ruin. Just up the road from our house.

***

END OF PART 1

Conclusion

I hope you have enjoyed this glimpse into the everyday triumphs and trials of my parents, Gladys and George Irving, and the wider Irving clan. Their story is more than a sequence of dates and events: it's the fabric of love, laughter, hardship and resilience that bound our family together through war, emigration, harsh winters and bright new beginnings.

If you've been moved by these diaries, you won't want to miss what comes next. In Book 2, you'll travel even farther back into my father's lineage, meeting his indomitable sea-captain forebear who survived two shipwrecks on the route between Canada and New York—and discovering how that branch of the Irving tree became tangled up in the notorious "Butterbox Babies" scandal of Nova Scotia. You'll see how courage, scandal and compassion shaped the men and women who raised my father, and learn how those experiences set the stage for the family's post-war journey.

And beyond that, Book 3 will bring my mother's side vividly to life: her father's service aboard HMS Hood before its fateful clash with the Bismarck in World War II; her grandparents' daring elopement from Amsterdam through Wales to Edinburgh; and even the astonishing tale of a distant cousin in Australia who claimed the Lithuanian throne.

Our family saga continues to unfold—more drama, more heartbreak, more humour, and above all more proof that ordinary lives can contain extraordinary stories. I very much hope you'll join me again for the next chapters of the Irving legacy. Thank you for reading.

Mum's Original Diary-Entries

1944

January

Farnborough

Saturday 1 Jan '44 – Moved from "Baveno" to "Victoria". No bed. Went up to Aldershot with George. Lt Irving has gone to London.

Sunday 2 Jan '44 – (Sunday) Moved from "Victoria" to "Fairview". No bed. Saw the film She Knew All the Answers (I never even knew the questions!).

Monday 3 Jan '44 – Collected my regimental mail (13–18–9). Nancy presses me to go to Tredenham House. Kit inspection (officer says, "What do you mean – you think it's at the laundry?"). Later I thought my underwear might be hanging up in Baveno. They were!

Tuesday 4 Jan '44 – Moved from "Fairview" to "Tredenham", into Nancy's room (there were four other beds; one girl, a minister's daughter, was always on her knees saying her prayers). Inoculation at 13:45. Blenheim cancelled. P/C. Met Lt Irving R.C.R. I didn't see much of him – George was in the way. On a shoe hunt. Bitter frost.

Wednesday 5 Jan '44 – Inoculation at 14:00. Spent 2/6 on soap, chocolate and cigarettes in the NAAFI. Blistered heels – new shoes. Saw the film Gentleman Jim Corbett. Walked back to the billet in socks.

Thursday 6 Jan '44 – Didn't sleep well. Shoes are giving me jip; so is the inoculation, and I still have that cold. Received two letters – answered one to Mum and one to Mum Irving.

Friday 7 Jan '44 – Pay parade £5 12 s. Went to the Toc H (Talbot House) library with George. He read Zane Grey; I read Edgar Wallace. Booked in at 10 pm.

Saturday 8 Jan '44 – Worked hard on annual-assessment pro formas; finished at 5 pm. Had supper in the café opposite Tredenham. Went to the Toc H (Talbot House) library; George lost his bicycle lamp.

Sunday 9 Jan '44 – (Sunday) Cycled with George to Fleet, Crookham, Odiham, Aldershot and Farnborough; then to Toc H (Talbot House) and the films The Adventures of Martin Eden and Confessions.

Monday 10 Jan '44 – Went with Joyce to White's to look at patterns. Cpl Burns is rigid about dust (am I cheesed!). Did washing and ironing (domestic evening). Duty clerk.

Tuesday 11 Jan '44 – Clothing parade: received tunic with G-i-C, skirt, three collars, tie and one pair of stockings.

Wednesday 12 Jan '44 – (S.T. in use). Sent home £3 for my bike to be forwarded; remainder to be used for birthday presents. Did ironing. Feeling low-spirited. Read W. W. Jacobs in Toc H (Talbot House) with George.

Thursday 13 Jan '44 – Nothing of interest. Saw the film Kings Row.

Friday 14 Jan '44 – Cpl Burns fussed again about the window. I asked the adjutant for ten minutes to return to Tredenham to open it; he refused. Saw Cpl Burns.

Saturday 15 Jan '44 – Very foggy and cold. Day off. Lent station bike to Rene. Went to lunch. Saw George at 1 pm. Went to Aldershot: bought two fountain pens at 12/6 each, one watch for 35 s, two birthday cards, ¼ lb cocoa, 6 d Bovril, torch battery and one bottle of Quink (1/6). Went to the Toc H (Talbot House) library. Cpl Norris (the "fat girl") on leave.

Sunday 16 Jan '44 – Breakfast, then to Group Office and back. Received card saying bike was despatched (very foggy and cold). Nancy returned from leave.

Monday 17 Jan '44 – Cpl Wynne in sick bay. Received two parcels (towel, sweets and magazine; bicycle pump and lamp). Domestic evening: stayed in and darned stockings. Invitation to Mrs Sims for Wednesday week.

Tuesday 18 Jan '44 – Collected my bicycle.

Wednesday 19 Jan '44 – Went with George to see Coney Island etc. it rained heavily.

Thursday 20 Jan '44 – Put my cap on the fireplace to dry; result was a nice design burnt into it. Went with Nancy to West Toc H (Talbot House).

Friday 21 Jan '44 – Received a letter from (ma-in-law) Irving; George did too. We sent an airgraph. George and I went to a dance with Nancy ("The Bucket").

Saturday 22 Jan '44 – Rain. Library.

Sunday 23 Jan '44 – Camberley with George; then to Toc H (Talbot House).

Monday 24 Jan '44 – Kit inspection. Did washing and ironing. Sent laundry to The Hampshire. Received three letters – from Lt Read, May Smylie and home.

Tuesday 25 Jan '44 – Got three pairs of shoes; wore a new pair to Toc H (Talbot House).

Wednesday 26 Jan '44 – Started work in Registry on "Outward Mail."

Thursday 27 Jan '44 – Busy.

Friday 28 Jan '44 – Busy.

Saturday 29 Jan '44 – Bought a present (tablemats for Cousin Lizzie, who's marrying a Canadian chap from N.S.).

Sunday 30 Jan '44 – Worked until 16:45. Loaned Nancy my bike.

Monday 31 Jan '44 – Busy.

February

Tuesday 1 Feb '44 – Went to Signals dance with George. Pretty good time.

Wednesday 2 Feb '44 – Went to the library.

Thursday 3 Feb '44 – Saw Walt Disney's Saludos Amigos.

Friday 4 Feb '44 – Wrote six letters and posted them.

Saturday 5 Feb '44 – Took Nancy to Toc H (Talbot House) with us.

Sunday 6 Feb '44 – Went cycling, then to the pictures. Met Cpl Byswater. Washed my hair.

Monday 7 Feb '44 – F.F.I., then did some washing. Went to West Toc H (Talbot House) with Eileen (from Bristol) and Nancy Tonkin. Had a bath. Parcelled up Lizzie's present (S.T. in use).

Tuesday 8 Feb '44 – Posted parcel and started work in P.3 section. Have got an awful cold. Went to see The Four Feathers with George. Received a letter from H. Read (Mrs Ross).

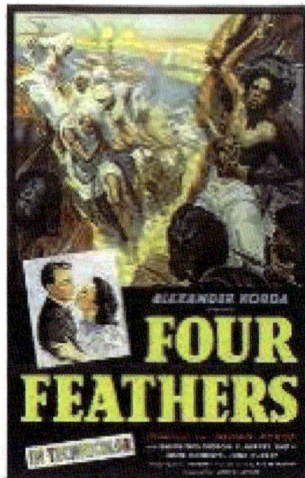

Wednesday 9 Feb '44 – (Full moon 05:29.) My cold is worse. Answered Helen's letters. A.C. Wallace wants his day pass (troublesome chap). Went to the library.

Thursday 10 Feb '44 – Wrote home. Went to the pictures with George to see Du Barry Was a Lady. Feel thoroughly sick with my cold. George gives me C.S.M.!

Friday 11 Feb '44 – (Lizzie W. married in RC church to Cpl Ross.) My cold is in its third stage. Mr Hewitt informs me that my attachment to P Staff will continue a few days after Mr Fraser's return.

Saturday 12 Feb '44 – Finished work at 15:30. Saw George at 16:30. Took the bus to Aldershot, came back, went to NAAFI and wrote letters. Saw Mr Fraser.

Sunday 13 Feb '44 – Got up for breakfast, then back to bed until 12:30. Saw George at 13:30. Had lunch. Went to La Scala, then Toc H (Talbot House).

Monday 14 Feb '44 – Domestic evening cancelled. Went to the Rex with George.

Tuesday 15 Feb '44 – Went to the M.T. dance in the Town Hall with George and Nancy (2 s). Saw Mr & Mrs Sims, who invited us to their home in Aldershot on Sunday. Letter from H. Ross.

Wednesday 16 Feb '44 – Mr Fraser back to work. Don't know how I stand—will I be moving out? Guess so. Letter from E. Langley. Heavy rain; parade cancelled.

Thursday 17 Feb '44 – Ordered zip bag, 41/6. Collected laundry.

Friday 18 Feb '44 – Duty clerk. Parcel from home and letter about Lizzie's wedding. Flight says, "You're coming upstairs in a day or two." Finished in P.3.

Saturday 19 Feb '44 – Submitted leave application A.D. 17/3 – 23:59 – 26/3/44 (9 days). Working in registry.

Sunday 20 Feb '44 – Visited Mrs Sims in Aldershot. Played gramophone and cards on the floor.

Monday 21 Feb '44 – Duty airwoman in Tredenham. Went to sleep and woke at 01:00, then back to bed. Answered phone at 03:00 and 06:00. Kit inspection (sent laundry in).

Tuesday 22 Feb '44 – On duty until 10:00. Went with George to see Dixie. Janet woke me for the raid, and Nancy spilt tea over me.

Wednesday 23 Feb '44 – Raid on. Went to …

Thursday 24 Feb '44 – Went to see They Met in the Dark.

Friday 25 Feb '44 – Went to the library. Worked in P.3 in the afternoon.

Saturday 26 Feb '44 – Day off. Went with Nancy to Guildford and with George in the afternoon to Aldershot. Saw Thank Your Lucky Stars.

Sunday 27 Feb '44 – Worked in P.3 in the morning and in the registry in the afternoon.

Monday 28 Feb '44 – Domestic evening. F.F.I. Went with Nancy to NAAFI; had sausage, beans and chips—and nightmares.

Tuesday 29 Feb '44 – Put in for my leave. Went cycling along the canal banks with George; enjoyed it very much.

March

Wednesday 1 March '44 – Two letters from home (one registered), and one from Elsie Langley. Bitterly frosty.

Thursday 2 March '44 – Chemical Warfare Day: we all dressed up. Went out at 18:30 to Toc H (Talbot House). Saw Sgt – small dark chap. Bright moonlight night. Collected two dance tickets (41 s).

Friday 3 March '44 – Collected laundry. Checked in cash at the P.O. Pay parade 34 s. Received a letter from Agnes and posted my reply.

Saturday 4 March '44 – Finished work at 15:30. Cycled through Aldershot. Toc H (Talbot House).

Sunday 5 March '44 – Rose at 10:00. Went cycling at 13:30. In bed at 22:00.

Monday 6 March '44 – Up at 07:15. Worked in the registry— O.K. by me. Duty clerk. Finished in P.3.

Tuesday 7 March '44 – At work in registry (stationery). Very tired at the dance.

Wednesday 8 March '44 – Working in stationery. To the theatre in the evening. Not awfully good.

Thursday 9 March '44 – Duty airwoman—what a bind. (My pass has been signed.)

Friday 10 March '44 – Met George and we went to the pictures to see So Proudly We Hail.

Saturday 11 March '44 – Finished at 16:30. Went to the pictures to see Stage Door Canteen at La Scala. Letter from Canada.

Sunday 12 March '44 – Went to NAAFI for breakfast (an orange). Went walking, then to Toc H (Talbot House) Had a boiled egg. No money.

Monday 13 March '44 – Letter from home. Sent laundry in. Locker inspection. Went to NAAFI. (I quit smoking—know why?)

Tuesday 14 March '44 – Clothing parade: 2 K, 1 stock, 1 collar.

Wednesday 15 March '44 – Went to the library and Toc H (Talbot House). Sent a letter home. Had a bath.

Thursday 16 March '44 – Got early chit for tomorrow. Packed my luggage and went to Toc H (Talbot House). We proceeded to argue.

Friday 17 March '44 – Must collect shoes (did). Off duty at 11:00. Pay parade 10:30 – £2 18 s. Shoes cost 5 s. Spent 5 s on papers. (Went on leave!)

Saturday 18 March '44 – Arrived Waverley Station at 05:00.

Sunday 19 March '44 – Went to see Aunt Liz with George (in uniform).

Monday 20 March '44 – George tried to fix the radio. Saw Betty Cavanagh—she's discharged from W.R.A.C. (know why?).

Tuesday 21 March '44 – Went to the Regal to see Lassie Come Home. Bought sweets in Woolworths.

Wednesday 22 March '44 – Bought gramophone for 45 s and records.

Friday 24 March '44 – Stayed home.

Saturday 25 March '44 – Left home at 07:50. Train from Waverley Station at 10:00.

Sunday 26 March '44 – Arrived King's Cross (London). Spent the day in St James's Park—lovely and warm. George bought me a compact.

Monday 27 March '44 – Back to work. Kit inspection and lecture (tripe). Collected 5 s on sweepstake.

April

Saturday 1 April '44 – Went to Farnham with Nancy.

Sunday 2 April '44 – Went cycling three hours.

Monday 3 April '44 – Duty airwoman. Bought the Nutcracker Suite, 19/11. Posted two Easter cards.

Tuesday 4 April '44 – Two chevrons. Went dancing.

Wednesday 5 April '44 – Pictures.

Thursday 6 April '44 – Did P.3, P.O.R.'s. Pictures.

Friday 7 April '44 – Had the afternoon off. Ate two hot-cross buns.

Saturday 8 April '44 – Answered letter home. Went to Can Y.M. Pictures. Put shoes in for repair.

Monday 10 April '44 – Letter from Sarah. No domestic evening. Went out.

Tuesday 11 April '44 – Terribly busy at the office. Stayed in in the evening.

Wednesday 12 April '44 – Still holding down two other jobs besides my own (one man off sick, the other away on leave).

Thursday 13 April '44 – Feel desperately tired. Got chocolate in C.Y.M.

Friday 14 April '44 – Got an assistant: Barbara Freeman (blonde). Letter from May Smylie.

Saturday 15 April '44 – Finished at 4 pm. Went to see Best Foot Forward. Changed shoes.

Sunday 16 April '44 – Miserable wet day. Rose at 7:00; back to bed at 8:30. Rose at 11:30 and went to lunch.

Friday 21 April '44 – Posted to R.A.E.

Saturday 22 April '44 – Reported to M.O.; put on light duties (know why?).

Sunday 23 April '44 – Heard cuckoo for the first time.

Tuesday 25 April '44 – Bought jumper and kimono, 20 s.

Wednesday 26 April '44 – Went for primroses with Nancy.

Saturday 29 April '44 – Bought five records, 5 s.

Sunday 30 April '44 – Finished work at 4 pm.

May

Monday 1 May '44 – Duty clerk. Handed in one shoe for repair.

Tuesday 2 May '44 – Went to the pictures Let's Face It.

Saturday 6 May '44 – Reported to M.O. to get discharge.

Friday 12 May '44 – Booked room in Harvey Hotel (now SeaviewEP) for two weeks from 15/5/44. Got cleared.

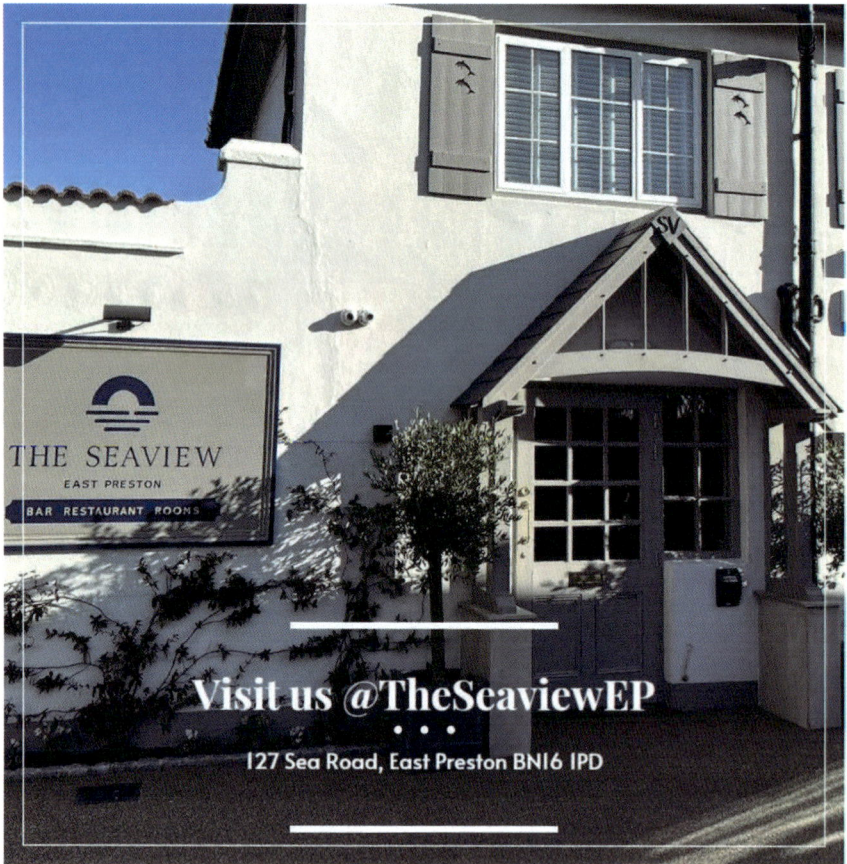

Harvey Hotel, now The SeaviewEP on the South coast of England

Saturday 13 May '44 – Finished cleaning of station.

Monday 15 May '44 – Moved into Harvey House.

Tuesday 16 May '44 – George gets pass.

Saturday 20 May '44 – Went with George to Guildford. Quaint old town. Visited fortifications of 43 B.C.

Sunday 21 May '44 – Went to see Always in My Heart. Went to bed after dinner.

Monday 22 May '44 – Bought 1 d pins, 1 d mint, 3 d coffee.

Saturday 27 May '44 – Bought tickets for Lilac Time with Nancy; the three of us went.

Sunday 28 May '44 – Effective date of discharge from WAAF. Said cheerio to Mrs — of Harvey House (£14).

Monday 29 May '44 – I travelled and arrived in Edinburgh at 7:00.

Tuesday 30 May '44 – Got ration cards etc.

June

Saturday 3 June '44 – Went to see Henry in the Haunted House.

Tuesday 6 June '44 – Doctors.

Saturday 10 June '44 – Went to Newton Grange.

Tuesday 13 June '44 – Went to Broxburn.

Wednesday 14 June '44 – One letter – George.

Saturday 17 June '44 – (Says here 1945!) George arrived in Halifax. Bought dressing table £6 6 s, maternity dress £3 3 s.

Monday 26 June '44 – Sure my heart's broken. He writes saying he thinks he'll take Nancy out to a show.

Tuesday 27 June '44 – Got 1 lb tomatoes. One letter from H. Read.

September

Sunday 17 September '44 – George and I went to the zoo.

November

Saturday 18 November '44 – Got mattress for the pram.

Thursday 23 November '44 – Letter from George says he's off to the Western Front.

Friday 24 November '44 – Telegram from George: off draft, broke. Send £3. Went in ambulance to maternity hospital.

Saturday 25 November '44 – Baby born 11:45 am, 8 lbs 11 oz (Frederick Walter).

Sunday 26 November '44 – Saw George and baby.

Wednesday 29 November '44 – George went to Newton Grange.

December

Monday 4 December '44 – Discharged from hospital.

Thursday 7 December '44 – George returned to his unit.

Tuesday 12 December '44 – Went to baby clinic; he weighs 9 lbs 9½ oz.

Printed in Dunstable, United Kingdom